Bob Chilcott

Furusato 故郷

5 MIXED-VOICE ARRANGEMENTS OF JAPANESE SONGS

日本の歌による５つの合唱曲（混声合唱用）

T0057082

MUSIC DEPARTMENT

OXFORD
UNIVERSITY PRESS

OXFORD
UNIVERSITY PRESS

Great Clarendon Street, Oxford OX2 6DP, England

Oxford University Press is a department of the University of Oxford.
It furthers the University's aim of excellence in research, scholarship,
and education by publishing worldwide

Oxford is a registered trade mark of Oxford University Press
in the UK and in certain other countries

© Oxford University Press 2011

Bob Chilcott has asserted his right under the Copyright, Designs
and Patents Act, 1988, to be identified as the Arranger of these Works

Database right Oxford University Press (maker)

First published 2011

All rights reserved. No part of this publication may be reproduced,
stored in a retrieval system, or transmitted, in any form or by any means,
without the prior permission in writing of Oxford University Press

Permission to perform the works in this anthology in public
(except in the course of divine worship) should normally be obtained
from a local performing right licensing organization, unless the owner
or the occupier of the premises being used already holds a licence
from such an organization. Likewise, permission to make and exploit a
recording of these works should be obtained from a local mechanical
copyright licensing organization

Enquiries concerning reproduction outside the scope of the above
should be sent to the Music Rights Department, Oxford University Press,
at the address above

Impression: 14

ISBN 978-0-19-337804-9

Music origination by Enigma Music Production Services, Amersham, Bucks.
Printed in Great Britain on acid-free paper by
Halstan & Co. Ltd, Amersham, Bucks.

Japanese translations by Miyako Hashimoto

Contents

Composer's Note / 作曲者の言葉 4

Sunayama (Sand Mountain) / 砂山 5

Mura Matsuri (Village Festival) / 村祭 9

Oborozukiyo (Hazy Moonlight) / おぼろ月夜 14

Furusato (Home Town) / 故郷 20

Momiji (Autumn Leaves) / 紅葉 24

Poems / 詩 30

Composer's Note

I have been very fortunate to come into contact with the fine and flourishing choral life of Japan through a number of visits to the country under the auspices of the Japan Choral Association. A very warm and happy relationship has also developed with Keiichi Asai and the Kyoto Echo Choir, and it is to them that I affectionately dedicate this set of arrangements of Japanese songs. I am very grateful to those at Pana Musica in Kyoto who suggested the selection of songs and to the poet Charles Bennett, who wrote the English singing translations. Thanks are also due to Tsuyoshi Chiba and to my friend from student days in London, Miyako Hashimoto, at whose suggestion I have dedicated the song 'Furusato' to the victims of the devastating Japanese earthquake of March 2011.

Bob Chilcott

日本合唱連盟との幸運な繋がりの下に幾度かに渡る来日を重ねる中で、日本の大変優れた、そして活発なコーラス界との関係を深めて来れたことを大変幸せに思います。この合唱曲集は、これまで友情を温め合って来た「合唱団京都エコー」と浅井敬壹さんに捧げます。曲目の選定についてご提案頂いたパナムジカ様と，英語の歌詞の作詞者のチャールズ・ベネットさんに心より感謝いたします。更に、出版に当たってお手伝い頂いた千葉剛さん及び学生時代よりの旧友の橋本美弥子さんにも、感謝の意を表させて頂きます。

ボブ・チルコット

Sunayama
砂山

Hakushu Kitahara (1885–1942)
English version by
Charles Bennett (b. 1954)

SHINPEI NAKAYAMA (1887–1952)
arr. BOB CHILCOTT (b. 1955)

© Oxford University Press 2011. Photocopying this copyright material is ILLEGAL.

14
S.
A.
T.
B.
p
mm
2. くれりゃすなーやま しおーなりばーかーり
2. Un - der our feet are sand dunes, un - der our feet the shift - ing sand.
18
すずめちーりーぢり またーかぜあーれる
Stars are blown like spar - rows, stars are flown on dark'n-ing wind.
22
みんなちりぢり もうーだれもみーえーぬ
Leaves on the storm we scat - ter, lost on the wing, no place to land.

*Keyboard reduction for rehearsal only.

34
oo
な ら あ ー し た う み よ さ よ な ら さ よ ー
sing a lul - la - by. Wa - ters ca - ress the shin - gle, breez - es
あ ー し た う み よ さ よ な ら さ よ ー な ら
lul - la - by. Wa - ters ca-ress the shin - gle, breez - es kiss be -
38
rit.
unis.
pp
p
な ら あ ー し ー た
kiss be - neath our wings.
あ ー し ー た ー
- neath our wings.

Mura Matsuri
村祭

English version by
Charles Bennett (b. 1954)

Trad. Japanese
arr. BOB CHILCOTT (b. 1955)

© Oxford University Press 2011. Photocopying this copyright material is ILLEGAL.

15
unis.
ドン ドン ヒャ ラ ラ ドン ヒャ ラ ラ
don don hya - la - la, don hya - la - la.
あ さ か ら き こ え る
Drum - ming in the ce - le - bra - tion,
19
ふ え た い こ
pi - ping in the joy!
24
f
T.
B.
2. と し も ほ う ね ん ま ん さ く で
2. We are the har - vest on the spread - ing vil - lage tree,

29
む ら は そ う で の お お ま つ り
We are the har - vest that is glow - ing in the sun.
33
f
S.
A.
ド ン ド ン ヒ ャ ラ ラ ド ン ヒ ャ ラ ラ ド ン ド ン ヒ ャ ラ ラ ド ン ヒ ャ ラ ラ
Don don hya - la - la, don hya - la - la, don don hya - la - la, don hya - la - la.
T.
B.
(f)
37
よ る ま で に ぎ わ う み や の も り
Drum-ming in the ce - le - bra-tion, pi - ping in the joy!
ff

42
ff
3. み の り の あ ー き に
3. We are ev - er thank - ful for the
ff

47
か み さ ま の め ぐ み た た え る む ら ま つ り
pro-mise of the year, Pour - ing your bless-ings on the peo - ple of the land.

53
ドン ドン ヒャ ラ ラ ドン ヒャ ラ ラ ドン ドン ヒャ ラ ラ ドン ヒャ ラ ラ
Don don hya-la-la, don hya-la-la, don don hya-la-la, don hya-la-la.

57
1.
2.
き いて も こ こ ろ が い さ み た つ い さ み た つ
Drum-ming in the ce-le-bra-tion, pi-ping in the joy! pi-ping in the joy!

Oborozukiyo
おぼろ月夜

Tatsuyuki Takano (1876–1947)
English version by
Charles Bennett (b. 1954)

TEIICHI OKANO (1878–1941)
arr. BOB CHILCOTT (b. 1955)

© Oxford University Press 2011. Photocopying this copyright material is ILLEGAL.

12
poco cresc.
り ひ う す れ
no - thing but a blur,
み わ た す や ま の ー は か ー
Those hills on the ho - ri - zon may be
poco cresc.
16
mp dolce
S.
A.
す み ふ か し
clouds for all I care.
は る か ぜ そ よ
The moon's a drown-ing
T.
B.
mp dolce
mp dolce
19
SOPRANOS
p
ふ ー く そ ー ら を み れ ば ゆ う
o - pal in a sky of cool - ing blue, The
p

22
S.
づ き か か り ー て に お い あ わ し
scent of spring u - pon the breeze has come to speak of you.
mp dolce
26
S.
(S.)
mp
ah
unis. mp
T./B.
2. さ と わ の ほ か げ ー も も ー
2. The win - dows of my vil - lage are a
ah
29
(A.)
mp
ah
poco cresc.
poco cresc.
り の い ろ も た な か の こ み
prim - rose glim - mer now, The dress you wore so
poco cresc.

32
mf dolce
か わ
And
ち ー を た ど る ひ と も
long a - go was like the moon when new.
mf dolce
35
ず の な く ね ー も か ー ね の お と
here's a bell that's roll - ing the time a - long its
mf dolce

38
ah
mp
も
tongue,
unis. mp
さ な が ら か す め ー る お ー
To tell me I must dance the moon as I
mp
41
mp
ah
p
poco tenuto
さ な が ら か す
To tell me I must
ぼ ろ づ き よ ー
did when I was young.
p
poco tenuto
p

45
a tempo
pp
め ー る お ー ぼ ー ろ づ き よ
dance the moon as I did when I was young.
oo
pp
a tempo
p
49
rit.
rit.
pp

2011年3月の東日本大震災と津波による
犠牲者の方々への追悼の為に

Furusato
故郷

Tatsuyuki Takano (1876–1947)
English version by
Charles Bennett (b. 1954)

TEIICHI OKANO (1878–1941)
arr. BOB CHILCOTT (b. 1955)

© Oxford University Press 2011. Photocopying this copyright material is ILLEGAL.

17
poco cresc.
mp
mm
め ー ぐ ー り ー て わ す れ が た き
run-ning in the moun-tains, My home is call - ing, is
mp
poco cresc.
mm
mp
mm
21
dim.
p
oo
ふ る さ と ー
call - ing to me.
oo
p
p
dim.
oo
oo
26
(p)
poco cresc.
2. い か に い ま す ち ち は
2. Fa - ther will sing in our gar - den a -
31
mp
dim.
は つ つ が な し や と も が
- gain, Mo - ther will smile like a blos - som - ing
oo
oo
mp
mp
oo
dim.
oo

35
p
poco cresc.
き
rose.
あ ー め に か ー ぜ に つ ー け ー
Voi - ces like rain - fall on mid - sum - mer's
p
p
あ ー め
Voi - ces
poco cresc.
39
mp
dim.
お も い い ず る ふ る さ
て ー も ー
As if the gar - den were call - ing my
eve - ning,
oo
mp
oo
mp
dim.
oo
oo
43
oo
p
dim.
と
name.
p
oo
oo
p
dim.
oo
48
pp
3. こ こ ろ ざ し を は た し て い つ の
3. Dream of to - mor - row and I shall be home, Home where my
pp
て い ー
home, Home

53
ひ に か か え ら ん や ー ま は
child - hood is wait - ing for me. Play - ing in the
ん や ー ー
me. Play - ing
57
あ ー お き ふ ー る ー さ ー と ー み ず は き よ き ー
wa - ter and run-ning in the moun - tains, My home is call - ing, is
62
poco rit.
a tempo
p
mm
ふ る さ と ー ー
call - ing to me.
み ず は き よ き ふ る さ
My home is call - ing, is call - ing to
p
p
mm
67
rit.
dim.
pp
mm
と ー
me.
mm
mm
mm
dim.
pp

Momiji
紅葉

Tatsuyuki Takano (1876–1947)
English version by
Charles Bennett (b. 1954)

TEIICHI OKANO (1878–1941)
arr. BOB CHILCOTT (b. 1955)

© Oxford University Press 2011. Photocopying this copyright material is ILLEGAL.

10
cresc.
い も ― か ず ― あ る な か に
turn - ing from a - pri - cot to um - ber.
cresc.
13
mf
S.
A.
ま ― つ を い ― ろ ― ど る ― か え ― で や ―
In the gold - en glow, the glow of late Sep -
T.
B.
mf
mf
16
dim.
mp
つ た は ― や ま の ふ も と の
- tem - ber, I see the moun - tain shi - ver,
dim.
mp
dim.
mp

19
す そーも よ う —
shi - ver and glim - mer.
p
23
mp espress.
2. た にのな が
2. Drift - ing on the
mp espress.
f dim.
mp espress.

26
れ に ち り ー う く も み ー じ
wind, on the wind of the stream,

29
cresc.
な み に ゆ ら れ ー て ー は な ー れ て
Lift - ed and re - leased in peach and
cresc.
cresc.

32
f
よ っ て あ ー か や き ー い ー ろ の ー
prim - rose, Just like a dress you wear, a
f
3
3
3
f
35
dim.
mp
い ろ ー さ ま ー ざ ま に ー み ず の う え
dress you wear once on - ly, Au - tumn is paint - ing
dim.
mp
3
3
dim.
mp

Processed in England by Enigma Music Production Services, Amersham, Bucks.
Printed in England by Halstan & Co. Ltd, Amersham, Bucks.

詩

砂山

作詞: 北原白秋
作曲: 中山晋平

一、　海は荒海
向うは佐渡よ
すずめなけなけ
もう日は暮れた
みんな呼べ呼べ
お星さま出たぞ

二、　暮れりや砂山
汐鳴りばかり
すずめちりちり
又風荒れる
みんなちりちり
もう誰も見えぬ

三、　かえろかえろよ
ぐみ原わけて
すずめさよなら
さよならあした
海よさよなら
さよならあした

村祭

文部省唱歌

一、　村の鎮守の　神様の
今日はめでたい　御祭日
ドンドンヒャララ
ドンヒャララ
ドンドンヒャララ
ドンヒャララ
朝から聞こえる　笛太鼓

二、　年も豊年　満作で
村は総出の　大祭
ドンドンヒャララ
ドンヒャララ
ドンドンヒャララ
ドンヒャララ
夜まで賑う　宮の森

三、　稔の秋に　神様の
めぐみたたえる　村祭
ドンドンヒャララ
ドンヒャララ
ドンドンヒャララ
ドンヒャララ
聞いても心が　勇み立つ

おぼろ月夜

作詞: 高野辰之
作曲: 岡野貞一

一、　菜の花畑に　入日薄れ
　　見渡す山の端　霞深し
　　春風そよ吹く　空を見れば
　　夕月かかりて　匂い淡し

二、　里わの火影も　森の色も
　　田中の小道を　辿る人も
　　蛙の鳴く音も　鐘の音も
　　さながら霞める　おぼろ月夜

故郷

作詞: 高野辰之
作曲: 岡野貞一

一、　兎おいし　かの山
　　小鮒釣りし　かの川
　　夢は今も　めぐりて
　　忘れがたき　故郷

二、　如何にいます　父母
　　恙なしや　友がき
　　雨に風に　つけても
　　思い出ずる　故郷

三、　志を　はたして
　　いつの日にか　帰らん
　　山は青き　故郷
　　水は清き　故郷

紅葉

作詞: 高野辰之
作曲: 岡野貞一

一、　秋の夕日に　照る山紅葉
　　こいもうすいも　かずあるなかに
　　松をいろどる　かえでやつたは
　　山のふもとの　すそもよう

二、　谷の流れに　散り浮く紅葉
　　波にゆられて　はなれてよって
　　赤や黄いろの　色さまざまに
　　水の上にも　織る錦